THE PIÑATA QUILT

Story◆Quilt Pattern◆Piñata Project

May life be filled
with piñatas
Enjoy

Jan Herran-Creamer

The Piñata Quilt
Copyright 1999 Jane Tenorio-Coscarelli
Publisher: ¼ Inch Designs & Publishing
Copy Editor: Jane Tenorio-Coscarelli
Translation Editor: Nicole Coscarelli
Quilt Designer: Jane Tenorio-Coscarelli
Machine Quilting By: Homespun Quilting by Debbie Jenks
Quilt Photography By: Carina Woolrich Photography

Published By
¼ Inch Designs & Publishing
39165 Silktree Drive
Murrieta Ca. 92563 USA

Library of Congress Cataloging Card Number: 99-64894
ISBN: HB 0-9653422-5-5
        PB 0-9653422-6-3

Printed in Hong Kong
By Regent Publishing Services

10 9 8 7 6 5 4 3 2 1

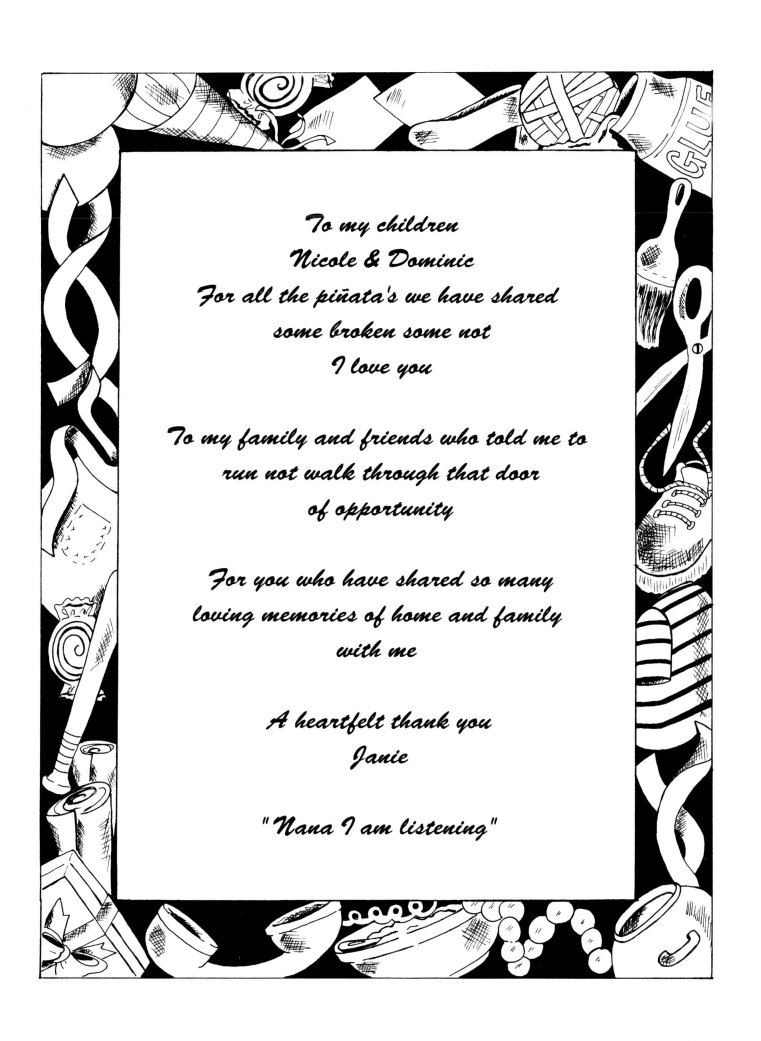

To my children
Nicole & Dominic
For all the piñata's we have shared
some broken some not
I love you

To my family and friends who told me to
run not walk through that door
of opportunity

For you who have shared so many
loving memories of home and family
with me

A heartfelt thank you
Janie

"Nana I am listening"

PIÑATA QUILT
STORY

In the early **morning hours,** Tia Lilly sat sewing the last **stitches** on the
horas de la mañana   *puntadas*

quilt she had been working on during so many **late nights**. "There
noches tardes

finished", she said to herself as she folded and placed the quilt into a

large box. Placing the lid onto the box she smiled, remembering the
caja grande

day her **nephew** came knocking on her front **door** so many **years** ago.
sobrino   *puerta*   *años*

Standing on his Tia's big **wooden porch**, Albert could barely stand still.
porche de madera

The thought of his **birthday** coming soon filled his body with
cumpleaños

excitement. His **loud knock** on the screen door announced his arrival.
golpe fuerte

He had come to ask his Tia to make a pinata for his birthday, which was

an important task for such a **small boy**. His Tia Lilly was a very clever
niño pequeño

lady, the official piñata maker and seamstress for the **family**. She would
familia

make the pinatas and sew all the **party dresses** for her nieces and
vestidos festivos

nephews birthdays, spending many **hours** at her sewing **table** cutting out
horas   *mesa*

tissue **paper** and cloth.
papel

"Who is it?" called Tia Lilly from the **kitchen**. "It's me Tia, Albert," he
                          cocina

replied, shouting through the screen door. "Oh Albert **how are you**?
                                                      ¿comó estás?

What brings my favorite nephew to **my door**?" asked Tia Lilly as she
                                  mi puerta

opened the door. "Come in. **Come in,**" she said. Albert followed her
 abrió   *Ven aquí*

into the kitchen.

11

He stood there nervously with his **hands** in his **pockets**. "Ah...Ah...Tia?"
manos   *bolsillos*

Albert mumbled. "**Yes?**" Tia Lilly replied, trying not to **laugh.** Albert
¿Si?   *reir*

looked down at the **floor**. "My birthday is coming Tia." he said "Oh yes,
suelo

your birthday is coming isn't it?" Tia replied, knowing exactly what he

was going to ask. "Yes" answered Albert."And you want me **to make**
hacer

you your piñata, don't you?" asked Tia Lilly, **smiling**. "Yes," replied a
sonriendo

now shy Albert. "Of course I will Albert. A birthday is not a **celebration**
fiesta

without a piñata". She looked at Albert's smiling **face**."You and I will go
cara

into **town** and pick out all the **paper** and **glue** we will need for your
ciudad   *papel*   *pegamento*

piñata." "And all the **candy** and **toys** too, Tia?" Albert asked.
dulces   *juguetes*

"Yes all the candy too my little one," Tia replied.

13

As they were **walking** down the **sidewalk** towards town, Tia Lilly turned
       caminando   *acera*

to Albert, and asked "What shall we make for your piñata? A **donkey**, a
                                                                       burro

cake, a **moon**, a **clown**?". Albert was quiet. This was a hard decision to
postre *luna*   *payaso*

make in just a **few minutes**. "A **star**!" Albert yelled out just a few
              pocos minutos *estrella*

moments later,"With bright, **colors. Red, green, blue, yellow** and
                        colores *rojo* *verde* *azul* *amarillo*

orange". "Okay" laughed Tia Lilly. "We'll make all the colors in the
naranja

rainbow."
arco

After they returned, Albert hurried and **unpacked** all the tissue **paper**
desempaqueto   *papel*

and **glue.** He separated the tissue paper on the table into piles by **color.**
pegamento   *color*

Tia Lilly brought in some **old newspapers**. "The newspapers will be our
periodicos viejos

first coat of the piñata." she said. Albert watched as his Tia showed him
primer

how to **cut the paper** into strips.
cortar el papel

Then she **mixed** the glue to make paste. "When I was a **little girl** my
mezcló   *niña pequeña*

father would take me into town and we would buy a **clay pot** for the
olla de arcilla

center of the piñata and then cover it with **paper**. Now we use a **balloon**
papel   *globo*

so it is not as heavy." We must have the paste just right, too much will

make the piñata too **hard** for someone to break," Tia said, as she **stirred**
fuerte   *agitó*

the glue mixture.

"Now dip the strips of paper in to the glue. **Cover** the whole balloon",
Cubre

she instructed. "Good Albert, you are doing a great job." When they

finished Tia Lilly told Albert that they must **wait** for the first layer to
espera

dry before they could add **three** or **four** more. "Come back **tomorrow**
secar   *tres*   *cuatro*   *mañana*

and we will put on another coat." "Okay" said Albert, as he **kissed** his
besó

Tia Lilly **good-bye.**
adíos

That day, Albert **walked home** with a skip in his step, thinking about all
caminó a su casa

the candy and **toys** they had bought for his piñata. He stopped and
los dulces   los juguetes

thought "If I add more glue to the piñata it will be too hard so no one

can **break** it I could have all the candy and toys to myself." He scratched
romper

his **head**, thinking some more. "Yes that's it!" he said.
su cabeza

Each day Albert returned to his Tia's **house** to work on the piñata. Every
casa

time his Tia left the **table** he would add more glue to the **paste.** The
la mesa   *el pegamento*

Piñata just got harder and harder. Finally they added the **star points** out
los puntos de la estrella

of cardboard and glued them to the **center**, then they decorated the
el centro

piñata with colored tissue paper.

Albert's **eyes** widen as he looked at his piñata "Oh it is so **beautiful**" he
ojos   _bonita_

shouted with delight. Each day Tia shared **stories** of all the piñatas the
los cuentos

family had shared. She **loved** to see the children **laughing** and
le gustó   _sonriendo_

screaming as they scrambled on the ground filling **bags** with candy and
gritando   _bolsas_

toys. "All this work is worth the looks on all your **faces** as someone
caras

breaks the piñata open. Will it be you Albert that breaks it this **year**?"
rompe   _año_

Tia asked. "I don't know" Albert replied, lowering his head.

The day of Albert's **birthday** finally came, and all the family and
cumpleaños

friends were there to **celebrate**. **Streamers** were hung and **party hats**
amigos   *celebrar*   *Las serpentinas*   *los sombreros festivos*

made. All the little girls wore their **best** party **dresses**, and everyone had
mejor   *vestidos*

brought **gifts**. Soon Albert's **mother** announced that it was time for the
regalos   *madre*

piñata. Albert's father tied a **rope** to the top of the piñata, making it
una cuerda

swing back and forth from the **patio** ceiling. All the children screamed
el patio

and wiggled with excitement. The **smaller children** went **first**. Albert's
los niños pequeñitos   *primero*

mother tied a **handkerchief** around their heads to cover their **eyes**. Then
un pañuelo   *ojos*

she spun them around while everyone **counted** out loud. **"One! Two!**
contaron   *Uno   Dos*

Three!" Albert's mother handed them the piñata **bat.** "Hit it! Hit it!"
Tres   *bate*

everyone yelled. Each **child** took a turn but no one could **break** the
niño   *romper*

piñata. The bat would just **bounce** off with each **swing**.
rebotar   *golpe*

Albert's **father** asked Tia Lilly "**Sister** what did you make this out of
      padre   *Hermana*

cement?" All the adults **laughed**, but not Tia Lilly. She was so
                    rieron

embarrassed, this had never happened before. "I am so sorry Albert I

have **spoiled** your birthday party with my piñata. I don't **understand**
    estropeado   *comprendo*

why no one can break it." But everyone just kept **laughing** at the **star** no
                                      riendo   *la estrella*

one could break.

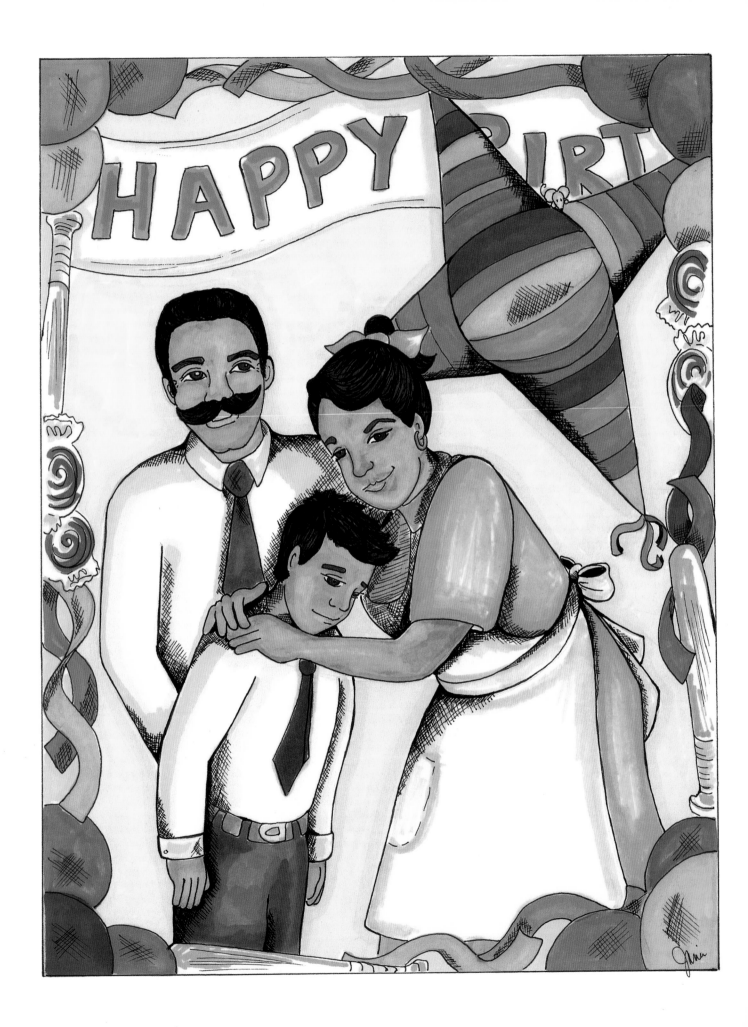

"**Stop** laughing!" yelled Albert "Stop! It's not Tia's fault it's mine. I put
Para

more glue into the **paste** to make it too **hard** to break so I could keep my
el pegamento   *fuerte*

star and all its **candy**." "You did what?" Tia asked with amazement on
dulce

her **face**. "I am so sorry Tia," Albert apologized. You'll never want to
cara

make me one again will you?" Tia **hugged** Albert. "That's okay I will
abrazo

always make you a piñata little one, always."

Albert's father went over to the star Piñata and cut some **small holes** in
pequeños agujeros

it with his pocket **knife**. "Okay Albert now hit it" his father shouted.
cuchillo

"Hit it! Hit it!"everyone yelled, and Albert did. Crack! Went the star and

a **shower** of candy and toys fell to the **ground**. Tia Lilly and Albert just
una ducha **el suelo**

smiled at each other. After they opened **presents** and **ate cake** and
sonrieron **los regalos comen postre**

ice cream, everyone laughed at the piñata no one could break.
helado

Years passed and many piñatas were broken each year. Albert was now
Años

too old for a piñata and had out **grown** the custom. As always **friends**
                          crecido   *amigos*

and **family** gathered to celebrate another birthday for Albert but this
familia

time he was **eighteen** and leaving soon for college. Tia Lilly entered the
             dieciocho

room with the **large box** and not a piñata under her **arm**. Albert, now a
el cuarto   *una gran caja*   *brazo*

tall young man, bent down to kiss his aunt's graying temples. "How is
alto

my **favorite** Tia?" Albert asked. **"Good, good**, Nephew."answered Tia
   favorita   **Bueno, bueno**

Lilly, as she sat down. "What is this you brought? A Gift? What no

piñata Tia?" Albert asked, as he started to **unwrap the box**. Tia smiled
                                     envolver la caja

"You are too old Albert, now open the box"

As Albert pushed through the **tissue paper** in the box, a **beautiful star**
papel de seda   *estrella bonita*

appeared. Everyone sighed as Albert held up his star quilt his Tia had

made. All the **colors** of the piñata no one could break, **yellow**, **red**,
colores   *amarillo rojo*

green and **blue**. "Tia it's my star" Albert whispered. "Yes" said Tia
verde   azul

Lilly "Remember the cement one?" Everyone **laughed**, especially Tia
rieron

Lilly and Albert.

Now, Albert takes all his **school books** off his **bed** after he finishes
libros de escuela   *cama*

studying for the **night**, uncovering the beautiful piñata quilt from
noche

underneath. Every time Albert looks at his quilt he remembers his Tia

Lilly and all the **birthdays** they shared together, along with the
cumpleanos

memories of growing up, and all the **smiles** she brought. But what he
memorias   *sonrisas*

remembers the most is the **day** that no one could break the piñata.
día

THE END

Did you find me on each page?

Directions - How to make a Paper Piñata

Materials

- Bottle Liquid Starch
- Newspapers- cut into 3 inch strips
- Tissue paper- Cut into 6 inch strips
- 1-Large balloon
- Water
- Glue
- Large Paint brush
- Paper scissors
- Light weight Cardboard
- Pie pan

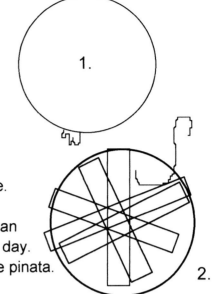

1. Blow up balloon to size wanted, tie knot on end set aside.
2. Mix starch 2 cups starch, 1/2 cup water in pie pan.
   Cut newspaper into 3" strips. Drip strips into starch pie pan
   and cover balloon surface completely. Set aside to day a day.
   Cut a small coat hanger and make a hook for hanging the pinata.
   Glue between layers of paper leaving hook end out..
3. Repeat to give balloon 3 coats of paper one each day.

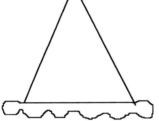

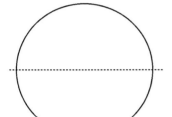 4a   b   c

4.a. With scissors cut 4- 8" half circles for cone shape from cardboard.
   b. Roll circles to create cone shape. Cut inch slits into base fold back
      to make a base. c. Glue onto dry piñata to make star points.
      Leaving one point open into center to stuff with candy later.
      Cover base ends with left over paper strips dipped in starch.
      Let dry. Pop balloon when shape is dry and firm.

Fold line

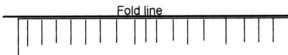

5. Cut tissue paper strips from different color paper.
   Fold strips in half length wise.
   On fold side cut inch deep and one inch apart.
   This will make a ruffle line. Turn open edge down
   and glue on to piñata making circle ruffle rows of color.
   Repeat until piñata is completely covered.
   Glue left over strips of tissue into the ends of piñata points.
6. Stuff piñata with candy, small toys, coins etc., Hang

PIÑATA QUILT

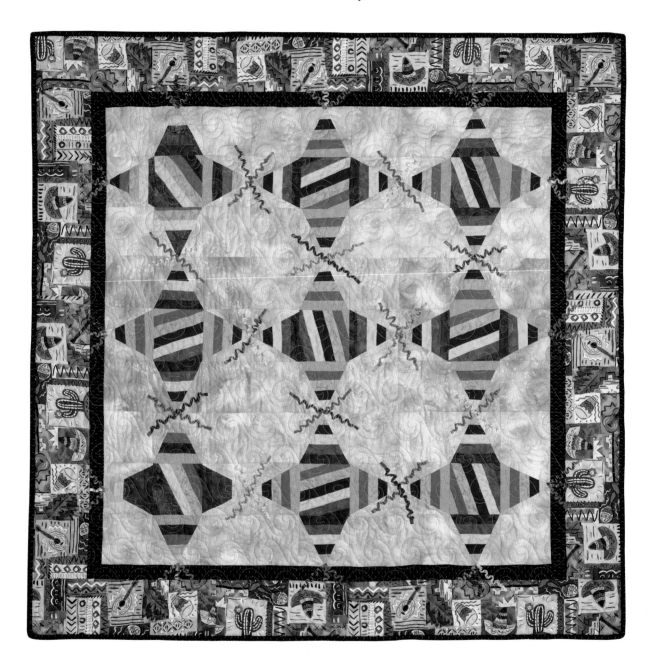

60" x 60"
Designed by Jane Tenorio
Quilted by Debbie Jenks

Piñata Quilt Instructions

Size 60" X 60"   9 Blocks-15" finished

Material: 1/3 Yd. -7 different bright fabric for piñata star strips

Yd..- alternate block background fabric

1/2 Yd.- border one and binding fabric

4 Yds...- backing fabric or 64" X 64"

62" x 62" batting

1 Yd. - border two fabric

Optional embellishment- 1 Yds- 1/4" ribbon of 6 different colors

Fabric reference for fabric used:

Star strip fabric- Quilter's Suede by Benartex Incorporated

Alternate block background- Fossil Fern by Benartex Incorporated

Outside border fabric- Mexicali by Alexander Henry Fabrics

Note: All cutting uses rotary cutting method and all piecing uses a 1/4 inch seam allowance

Piecing method

A. Paper piece- Paper piece the block using pattern provided.

B.. Foundation piece- Strip piece the piñata points. Then foundation piece them onto muslin or paper.

1. Cut 2- 1 1/2 " strips of each color star fabric. Sew seven together in a row. Press

1.    2.    3.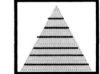

2. Trace and cut out center triangle adding seam allowance to template.

3.   Sew center strip to center of foundation piece.

Cut outside corner pieces sew to sides of triangle right sides together. Sew 36 star point units.

4. Cut 9- 5 1/2" center star square using template.

Adding seam allowance to template.

Placing pattern on an angle on strip piece.   4.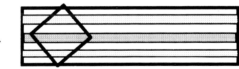

5. Cut 36- 5 1/2" alternate squares. Sew to each side of star points see layout.

Repeat blocks to complete 9- 15 1/2" pieced stars.

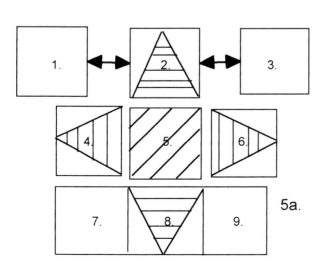

5a.

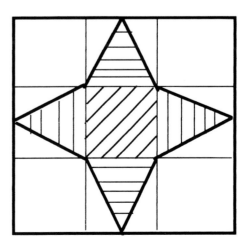

5b.

45

Center Top

Sew all 9 blocks together for quilt center.
Matching star points. Press square up.

Border One

Cut 2 strips- 46"x 2" sew to side of center
Cut 2 strips- 48 1/2"x 2"
Sew to top and bottom of center. Press
(Remember to re-measure your borders
before cutting fabric and square up all sides)

Border Two

Cut 2 strips- 4"x 48 1/2" sew to side of
quilt top. Press
Cut 2 strips- 4"x 60" Sew to top and bottom
of center. Press

Finishing

Layer backing, batting and quilt top Baste in place.
Hand or machine quilt (refer to basic quilt book
for directions if needed.) Bind using any method you prefer.

Optional Ribbons Embellishment:

To make streamers, cut 6 - 1/4 inch ribbon strips, 3 for each star point.
Hand sew to top of quilt at each star point. Refer to photo for placement

Piñata Quilt Layout

Piñata Quilt Paper Piecing Pattern

4 Points for each star block= 36 total

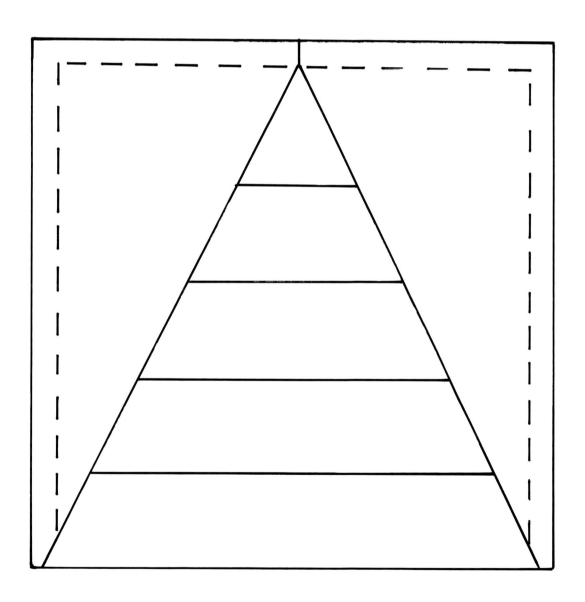

(Remember to add seam allowance if drafting templates)

Other Products from ¼ Inch Designs & Publishing

Books
The Tortilla Quilt
The Tamale Quilt
The Ants / Las Hormigas

Quilt Patterns

Coffee Girls	And Baby Makes Three	Raggedy Pals
Cat's Pajamas	Material Garden	Teas the Season
Deck the Cat	A Box of Chocolates	Heart of My Heart
Okay Corral	Roller Ghoster	Harvest Moon
Fall Friends	Winter Willie	Spring Seeds
Summer Picnic	Cooped Up	Mending Hearts

Doll Patterns
Maria Doll   Quilt-a-beast Doll

Other Products
Quilt-a-beast Mugs & Tote Bags
Fall & Winter Note Card Sets

**For author visits, lectures, workshop information
or to order contact:**

¼ Inch Designs & Publishing
39165 Silktree Drive, Murrieta Ca. 92563
Phone 909 677-5915 Fax 909 696-5699 E-mail: Quarteri@aol.com
For a catalog send a SASE